To Brian Moses and Gaby Morgan,
who helped start my poetry adventure
R.S.

To Eddie, the collie-shaped hole in my life
M.S.

Text copyright © Roger Stevens 2022

Not Much to Look At first published in 2022. All other poems
have been previously published by Macmillan Children's Books
in Roger Stevens' solo collections (*I Did Not Eat the Goldfish,*
Why Otters Don't Wear Socks, The Monster That Ate the Universe,
Beware! Low-flying Rabbits Ahead) and in anthologies.

Illustrations copyright © Mike Smith 2022

Designed by Steve Wells

First published in Great Britain and in the USA in 2022
by Otter-Barry Books, Little Orchard, Burley Gate, Herefordshire, HR1 3QS
www.otterbarrybooks.com

A catalogue record for this book is available from the British Library.

ISBN 978-1-91307-441-8

Illustrated with line drawings
Printed in Great Britain
9 8 7 6 5 4 3 2 1

For Lucy

RAZZ MA TAZZ

THE POETRY WORLD OF
ROGER STEVENS

ILLUSTRATED BY MIKE SMITH

Otter-Barry BOOKS

Roger Stevens

CONTENTS

THE WORLD OF PETS

NURSERY RHYME FUN

IF I COULD BE SERIOUS FOR A MOMENT

THE FUN OF BEING A POET

WORLD OF THE WILD

FUNNY HA HA

SOME OF MY FAVOURITES

HOW TO READ THIS BOOK

A poetry book can be read in a slightly different way to a story book. The basic reading method is the same, though, for both. Have the book in front of you and make sure it's the right way up. It should open so that you can turn the page towards you, and over. It's best to be sitting comfortably with the book in front of you, at just the right distance away to make reading it fairly easy. You may read it lying down, or standing up. But I'd recommend NOT reading it while in the shower, playing football or walking the dog, or the cat, or the hamster.

Unlike a storybook you may open this book at any page and read what you find there. The poems don't have to be read in order. Although I must point out that I've taken ages arranging them in a pleasing way. So I would quite like you to start at the front. But you don't HAVE to. Also, sometimes poems sound better if you read them out loud. Give it a try.

I like performing my poems in schools and libraries and at festivals. So I've imagined that I am standing right in front of you, reading the poems to you. And just like I do when I'm performing, I often tell you something about the poem; maybe how I came to write it, or how you could perform it.

Oh, and I've included one or two useful tips for writing poems of your own. Have fun.

Roger Stevens

FREQUENTLY ASKED QUESTIONS

Why don't poems always rhyme?
Because poems love making a fuss
They don't like sitting quietly
Although this one does

Where do you get your ideas from?
They come to me in the night
I keep an ideas trap by my bed
And gloves - in case they bite

What is the best poem you ever wrote?
It was called Seven Ways to Eat Fudge
But was stolen one day and sold on eBay
By a rival who bore me a grudge

What is your favourite word?
I like *crunchy* and *fizzle* and *toast*
Carpet sure takes some beating
But I think I love loving the most

Why was poet your chosen profession?
At rounding up words I was skilled

If you weren't a poet, what would you be?
Unhappy, unhinged, unfulfilled

What advice can you give to young poets?
This advice if you want to succeed
Read, read, read, read, read, read, read
Read, read, read and read

(And read! Did I mention that?)

THE WORLD OF SCHOOL

OUR NEW TEACHER

Last Christmas our teacher went skiing
Leaping from glaciers with glee
She sped down the snow like a bolt from a bow
But she couldn't get on with 6B

At Easter she sailed around Iceland
On a stormy and dangerous sea
Incredibly brave, she rode a huge wave
But she just couldn't handle 6B

In summer she went pony-trekking
From Argentina into Brazil
Paddling a canoe down the Iguazu
But 6B made her feel ill

Now 6B have left for the big school
And Teacher has us in her charge
It's exciting and fun to hear all she has done
And we're all well behaved – by and large

So we asked, "Do you miss your old class, Miss?"
And she went all quiet and sad.
Then her face lit up and she started to laugh.
"What, me? Miss 6B? Are you mad?"

TEACHER, TEACHER

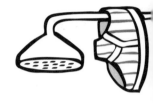

Teacher, teacher
If you can't find Sue
She's in the cloakroom
Looking for her shoe

Teacher, teacher
If you can't find Ben
He's in with the Head
Cos he's late again

Teacher, teacher
If you can't find Hans
He's still in the shower
Cos he's lost his pants

*You might be very surprised to know how many odd
things, as a teacher, I've found left behind in showers
and swimming-pool changing rooms. Including shoes,
trousers and, yes, pants.*

WE ARE THE COOL

We're Year Six boys
And we are The Cool
The coolest class
In the school

We don't smile
We don't make a fuss
There's no one as cool
As cool as us

We stand in the playground
We talk about stuff
We walk very slowly
Because we are tough

We saunter, we hang
We are nobody's fool
We're the boys in Year Six
And we are The Cool

*I like performing this in schools because I can watch
the lower year students peering round to see how the
year 6s react. Some boys are a bit embarrassed but, as
you will know if you are in year 6, mostly they are cool!
And Year Six girls seem to enjoy the poem on the
next page!*

YEAR SIX SISTERS

We are the Year Six Girls
We are the Year Six Crowd
We are the Year Six Posse
We are the Girls Out Loud

We are the Year Six Sisters
And we know how to have a laugh
We scare the Year Six boys for sure
And they don't dare cross our path

The teachers say we're a dream to teach
But they haven't got a clue
In lessons we're quiet and well behaved
If only the teachers knew

That we're passing notes and swapping jokes
And discussing various ploys
To humiliate and irritate
And generally wind up the boys

We are the Year Six Posse
The girls of intellect
We are the Year Six Sisters
So treat us with respect

LOUDER

Okay, Andrew, nice and clearly,
off you go.

WELCOME EVERYBODY TO OUR SCHOOL CONCERT....

Louder, please, Andrew.
Mums and dads won't hear you at the back, will they?

WELCOME EVERYBODY TO OUR SCHOOL CONCERT...

Louder, Andrew. You're not trying.
Pro -
    ject -
        your -
            voice.

Take a b i g b r e a t h and
louder!

WELCOME EVERYBODY TO OUR SCHOOL CONCERT...

For goodness sake, Andrew.
LOUDER!   LOUDER!

WELCOME EVERYBODY TO OUR SCHOOL CONCERT

Now, Andrew, there's no need to be silly.

This is a great favourite, and so much fun to perform. I've seen some brilliant videos of this being performed, from all over the world. One person plays the teacher and one plays Andrew. The trick, when performing this, is to really go for it. Be very quiet in the quiet bits and VERY LOUD at the end. I mean, REALLY LOUD. Oh, and, like all performances, don't rush it. Give the audience room to laugh.

CORRECTIONS

Teacher said,
Leave out the the,
two too's one too too many
and and after the comma
should go after the any.

The the, the too
and move the and
and that should make it flow.
Not that that, that that's fine –
but this that, that could go.

I said,
The the, the too, the and –
I would agree with you.
But I'm very fond of that –
this that and that that too.

Which that is that?
Is that this that?
Asked Teacher with a grin.
Okay but take that last in out
And leave that last out in.

I thought it would be fun to write a poem and see how many times I could write the same word next to itself and still make sense. It's fun to perform, too.

INTRODUCING DAD

If I may, Miss,
I'd like to introduce my dad.
Mum left us last year
and that made him really sad.
He told me you were pretty
and his favourite colour's beige,
and it isn't that uncommon
to date women half your age.
And we all know that he's bald
beneath that funny flick of hair,
you just have to humour him
and pretend his hair's all there.
His feet smell a bit funny
and his brain's a trifle slow.
But you haven't got a boyfriend, Miss,
so...

could you please give Dad a go?

CHICKEN SCHOOL TIMETABLE

Period one – simple clucking

Period two – more clucking

Period three – clucking with attitude

Period four – clucking with indecision

Period five – pecking in dirt

Period six – pecking in gravel

Period seven – rhythmic and jerky neck movements

Period eight – clucking (revision)

Why shouldn't chickens go to school? This is fun to perform. Working in a group of four, one person is the narrator and reads out each line. The other three are the chickens, performing the action. You can have great fun making up lessons for other unusual schools too. For example – School for Monkeys, School for Robots or School for Zombies.

TEACHER, TEACHER

(Alternative version)

Teacher, teacher
Millicent Witt
Has hidden the hamster
In her PE kit

Teacher, teacher
Jeremy Pear
Has hidden Beth's socks
And he won't tell her where

Teacher, teacher
Alasdair Tup
Says these rhymes are contrived
And the names are made up

THE WORLD OF FAMILY

DRUM KIT FOR SALE

Drum Kit For Sale
Guaranteed to make house shake

Very Loud Indeed

(Gave Mum a headache)

Drum Kit For Sale
Snappy snare – terrific tone
Dad says – must go at any price

(or will exchange for trombone)

When I was eight I made a drum kit out of biscuit tins,
an old broken doll's pram and dustbin lids, all of which
I hit with wooden sticks. I played it at the top of our
garden. I'm surprised the neighbours didn't complain.
It was very loud.

DAD, DON'T DANCE

Whatever you do, don't dance, Dad
Whatever you do, don't dance.
Don't wave your arms
Like a crazy buffoon
Displaying your charms
By the light of the moon
Trying to romance
A lady baboon
Whatever you do, Dad, don't dance.

When you try to dance
Your left leg retreats
And your right leg starts to advance
Whatever you do, don't dance, Dad
Has a ferret crawled into your pants?
Or maybe a hill full of ants
Don't Samba
Don't Rumba
You'll tumble
And stumble
Whatever you do, Dad, don't dance.

Don't glide up the aisle with a trolley
Or twirl the girl on the till
You've been banned from dancing in Tesco's
Cos your tango made everyone ill.
Whatever you do, don't dance, Dad
Whatever you do, don't dance.

Don't make that weird face
Like you ate a sour plum
Don't waggle your hips
And stick out your bum
But most of all – PLEASE –
Don't smooch with Mum!
Whatever the circumstance.
Whatever you do –
Dad, don't dance.

This is one of my most-requested poems. When I visit schools I ask whose dad or stepdad can dance. And very few hands go up. Then I ask: whose dad thinks he can dance? Almost every hand goes up. In case you're wondering, of course, I am a very good dancer!

MY STEPDAD IS AN ALIEN

I'd suspected it for some time.
I finally got up the courage
to talk to him about it.

I think you're an alien.

Nonsense. Why do you think that?

You're bald. You don't have any hair
anywhere.

That's not unusual. Lots of men are bald.

Well, you've got one green eye
and one blue one.

That doesn't make me an alien.

You can make the toaster work
without turning it on.

That's just a trick.

Sometimes I hear you
talking to Mum in a weird alien language.

I'm learning Greek
and Mum lets me practise on her.

What about your bright blue tail?

Ah...
You're right, of course.
So, the tail gave it away, did it?

When I went to live with Jill, who is now
my wife, her son, Joe, was very young. One
evening he took her to one side and asked
her, very seriously, if I was an alien.
I don't know how he found out. I thought I'd
hidden the fact very cleverly. He didn't tell
me about this until he was grown up.

COUSIN

This summer
A distant cousin came to stay
But I didn't see him
He was too far away

MESSAGES
AT SCHOOL

When I'm feeling low
I whisper a secret message into my hand
and hold it tightly in my fist
until playtime.
Then I release my message,
watch it soar
like a carnival balloon
into the speckled sky.
At night,
when Mum has turned out the light,
I think of Dad
and I'm sad that he's dead,
but I still have the message
he whispered to me.

I pick up the conch shell
by my bed
and listen again.
I hear him,
like the echo of a shooting star
in the seas of space.
Don't worry, he whispers,
I love you.

TREASURE TRAIL

Normally
I get home from school
and go straight out again
to the park
but today

I spotted a penny on the hall floor
and as I bent to pick it up
I spotted another –
one pace away.

As I bent to pick that up
I spotted another –
one pace away.

As I bent to pick that up
I spotted yet another
on the bottom step
of the stairs.

I picked it up
and spied another
on the third step

and another on the seventh
and another on the tenth
and another at the top.

At the top of the stairs
I spotted a five p
on the landing –
one pace away.

At this rate I was going to be rich.
I followed the trail
to the door of my room.

The door was open
and I could see
a ten p
on my floor.

I went in and,
as I bent to pick it up,
the door slammed shut
behind me.
I tried to open it
but it was shut fast.
A note was pinned to the door.

It said, *You are my prisoner.*
You are not getting out
until you have tidied your room!
Signed
Mum

And all for
twenty-five p!

MOTHER'S DAY PRAYER

Dear God,
Today is Mother's Day.
Please make her back-ache go away.
May her pot plants all grow healthy
and a lottery win make her wealthy.

May our Dad buy her some flowers
and take us all to Alton Towers.

May her sponge cake always rise
and the sun shine bright
in her blue skies.

Protect her, God, from every storm
but most of all
please keep her warm.

*My mum was always cold. Even in summer. I've a lovely
picture of her and Dad sitting on the beach in deckchairs
and she's wearing a big, heavy coat.*

MUM'S GRAVE

It's in a quiet and peaceful spot, I guess
It's made of marble
There are trees, dead leaves and grass

And by the headstone is a wooden letterbox
Where we can post our memories
I don't use it a lot
I mainly say a prayer
And let it rise into the cloudy sky
Above Mum's grave
Because she's not down there

Mum's grave is just a line
That's written underneath the word goodbye

MUM & DAD

Tenderskin & Roughchin

Dawngreeter & Toastjuggler

Cuddlebear & Grizzlybear

Firmhand & Strongarm

Sadsmile & Grinner

Busybee & Grasshopper

Spicegrinder & Potstirrer

Sunsoaker & Ballspinner

Spidershrieker & Jarcatcher

Taleteller & Dreamweaver

Earthmother & Earthmover

THE WORLD OF PETS

WALKING THE DOG
SEEMS LIKE FUN TO ME

Dad said, The dog wants a walk.
Mum said to Dad, It's your turn.
Dad said, I always walk the dog.
Mum said, Well I walked her this morning.
Dad said, She's your dog,
I didn't want a dog in the first place.
Mum said, It's your turn.

Dad stood up and threw the remote control
at the pot plant.
Dad said, I'm going down the pub.
Mum said, Take the dog.

Dad shouted, No way!
Mum shouted, You're going nowhere!
I grabbed Judy's lead
and we both bolted out the back door.

The stars were shining like diamonds.
Judy sniffed at a hedgehog, rolled up in a ball.
She ate a discarded kebab on the pavement.
She chased a cat up a tree.

Walking the dog
seems like fun to me.

HAMMY HAMSTER'S GREAT ADVENTURE

He was sitting on Granny's hand
when he noticed the opening
between the sleeve of her blouse
and her arm
and decided to investigate....

Granny said,

Ooh
Aah
Eeek
No!
Ouch!
Ooooooooh
Ha!
Hee hee hee
Ah
Ah
No... no...
Ouch!
Mmmmmmmm
Eek
Ugh!
Aaaaaaaaaaaaaaahhhh...
Ah...

And Hammy,
emerging from Granny's left trouser leg,
said,
Hmmm – that was interesting.
I think I might try it again.

Another great poem to perform. Use lots of actions as you mime Hammy travelling under your clothes. Don't worry about getting the sounds exactly as I've written. Just imagine the sounds you would make if a hamster was crawling up your sleeve and out of your trouser leg.

PETS

I have a pet dragon
His name is Dai
But no one ever sees him
Cos he's very, very shy

I have a pet iguana
His name is Stu
I don't suppose you'll ever meet him
Cos he lives in Peru

I have a pet spider
His name is Fred
You can see him if you like
But he's a little bit dead

SECRET

You can bribe me with treats
and biscuits and meats,
but I'm not telling you
where I buried it.
You can yell, you can shout,
you can stomp all about,
but I'm not telling you
where I buried it.

You can stroke me and tickle me
under my chin,
you can say, "Just you wait
till your mummy gets in."
You can offer me caviar
straight out of the tin,
but I'm not telling you
where I buried it.

It's my favourite toy.
It's what gets my vote.
I just love to chew it.
It's what floats my boat.
I don't know what it's for
but it's called "a remote".
And I'm NOT telling you
where I buried it.

FAREWELL, PETE

I had a little dinosaur
Nothing would it eat
But a chocolate cupcake
And my best mate, Pete

At school it burst the football
It wasn't fond of sports
It gobbled up the goalposts
And Mr Walton's shorts

It chased my Auntie Emma
You should have heard her shout
But it didn't like my granny
In fact, it spat her out

MOBILE HOME FOR SALE

Judy is a delightful

Mobile Home

with Central Heating

a warm Basement

superb Penthouse views

and includes luxury

Deep Pile Carpets

in black and white.

Fully Air-Conditioned

by large wagging tail.

This Border Collie

would suit large family of fleas.

STICK

It might seem obvious to you humans

But it puzzles me every day

If you want the stick so badly

Why do you throw it away?

This was the first poem that my dog, Judy, wrote. I had been walking along the beach trying to think of rhymes for sea. When I got home I found this poem on my desk. Dogs don't usually write things as their paws can't hold a pen. But it turned out that Judy had written it using the laptop keyboard. She was a very intelligent dog.

HOLE

There is a hole
In the space around me
You can't see it
But it goes everywhere with me
It's Border Collie shaped
And it doesn't come when it's called

For it's a hole
It's empty
And it's not called Judy

*You may have noticed that I wrote a poem for my mum
after she died and for my dad. This one was for Judy.
When somebody you love or a pet dies, it's just about the
saddest time there can be. So I like to write a poem about
it. It's a way to express your feelings and I think it helps
you feel just a little bit better. And also, when I read the
poem, years later, it reminds me of the person, or the pet,
with fondness and maybe a little smile.*

NURSERY RHYME FUN

ROCK-A-BYE BABY

Rock-a-bye baby
On the tree top
When the wind blows
The cradle will rock
When the bough breaks
The cradle will fall
What a stupid place to put the baby!

JACK AND JILL - A SONNET

The moon doth shine as bright as in the day.

I sit upon the see-saw wondering why

She left me. Boys and girls come out to play.

But I'm bereft. I think I'm going to cry.

I gave her chocolate and I praised her skill

At skateboarding and football not to mention

Arm wrestling. As we slowly climbed the hill

To fetch some water, did I sense a tension?

She seemed preoccupied. She hardly spoke

And as we turned the handle to the well

I asked her, Jill, please tell me it's a joke.

She said, I've found another bloke. I fell,

I rolled, head over heels into the dark,

Down to the bottom where I broke my heart.

PETER PIPER

(Easy Version)

Peter Piper chose a large number
of peppers that had been soaked in vinegar and
spices

A large number of peppers
that had been soaked in vinegar and spices
was chosen by Peter Piper

If it is indeed true
that Peter Piper chose a large number
of peppers that had been soaked in vinegar and
spices

where are they?

*I think this is an improvement on the original
tongue-twister, don't you?*

HEY DIDDLE DIDDLE

Hey diddle diddle
The cat and the fiddle
The cow jumped over the bed
The little dog laughed
But not for long
Cos the cow landed right on his head

THE OWL AND THE PUSSYCAT

The Owl and the Pussycat

Went to sea

The Owl ate the Pussycat

Oh dearie me

WHOOPS

A million little dinosaurs
Having a good time
One fell over a cliff
And then there were
Nine hundred and ninety-nine thousand,
nine hundred and ninety-nine.

Nine hundred and ninety-nine thousand,
nine hundred and ninety-nine dinosaurs
Having lots of fun
An asteroid hit the Earth
And then there were none.

IF I COULD BE SERIOUS FOR A MOMENT

A FOOTBALLER'S PRAYER

Dear God

Please bless my feet

May they kick the ball

"Real sweet!"

Keep my balance

Keep me on my toes

Help my team-mates

Outfox my foes

May my feet

March to victory

Win the match and the double

And may my feet always

Walk away from trouble

WHAT'S MY NAME?

I'm the sun that lights the playground before the
work begins

I'm the smile when Teacher cracks a joke. I'm the
giggles and the grins

In assembly I'm the trophy that the winning team
collects

In your maths book I'm the page of sums where
every one's correct

I'm the pure blue sky and leafy green that wins the
prize in art

I'm steamy, creamy custard dribbling down the
cook's jam tart

I'm the noise of playtime rising through the
stratosphere

I'm the act of kindness when you lent your kit to
Mia

I'm the star you were awarded for your startling
poetry

I'm the school gates swinging open on the stroke of
half-past three

If you look for me, you'll find me. What's my name?
Can you guess?

I live just round the corner and my name is

Happiness

SADNESS

I am the click of the catch
The heavy clunk
Of the closing door

The final words that hang in the air

The precious seconds of stillness

Before my mother starts crying
Before she grabs my hand
Before the carriage jerks and moves
Before my father half smiles at me, half waves

And the train leaves the station forever

A great way to write a poem about emotions is to imagine the emotion itself is telling the poem. That's how I wrote these two poems. Imagine Happiness or Sadness is a person and you are asking the person to describe himself or herself. Try it with Loneliness or Jealousy or Anger. For example, with Anger, I am a volcano of red hot lava exploding into a clear blue sky...

A WEEK OF HAIKUS

1
Plate on the table
Bird in the cherry blossom
Escapes from my hand

2
Upon still water
a flash of gold and turquoise
The dragonfly's gone

3
There is a tension
as bees and beetles struggle
on the pool's surface

4
Was that a donkey?
Or did some monster lung just
swallow a trumpet?

5
One, two, three, four, five
accumulating darkness
crow keeps his counsel

6

The wind shakes the school
like the beat of a dragon's wing
on a winter's night

7

A large black beetle
crash-lands on the cool floor tiles
and wonders, What now?

*I usually use the term "haiku-style" when talking about
these poems. A genuine haiku is much more than a poem
with just three lines and seventeen syllables, and is very
difficult to write. There are so many rules, far too many
to list here. Let's just say that a haiku usually refers to
nature, is quite serious and should contain a reference
to the season.*

THE MUSEUM SAYS

Be awed as you climb my heavy stone steps. Built
to last.

I am old by your standards. Two hundred years
have rolled past.

But young by the measure of all of the treasure I
hold.

My tomes tell of kingdoms long gone in vast
rooms of old gold.

My pillars of marble reach up to the cold
winter sky.

And my heart is of granite.

A dinosaur sleeping am I.

THE ART GALLERY SAYS

Hey, I'm cool.
My lines *sweep*. **Zoom**.
Catch the eye.
They turn beneath
a fresh spring sky.
groovy textiles.
Razzmatazz.
This year's black.
I'm now.
H I P .
Jazz.
My wood is polished.
I have awkward seats.
Ergonomic.
White walls with crazy
coloured blue and red paintings.
MANIC.
I am a bird about to rise
into the clouds.
Organic.

SHOUTING AT THE OCEAN

There's no point shouting at the ocean
When you're feeling low
The tide will still come in
It doesn't want to know

It's no good shouting at the ocean
Just because it's there
You can yell, throw stones or kick the sand
The ocean doesn't care

There's no use railing at the ocean
If you're angry or upset
The sea won't even notice you
It's too busy being wet

For the sea has no emotion
It doesn't hear you shout
It only listens to the moon
It just comes in and out

So if you're hurt, upset or angry
Write down all you want to say
Then post it in the ocean
Watch your troubles float away

THE FUN OF
BEING A POET

WHO SAYS A POEM ALWAYS HAS TO RHYME?

There was a young man called Frank
Who kept his pocket money in the... *

When he'd saved enough he bought an electric viola
And celebrated with a can of co... **

When he plays the viola the whole house rocks
It makes your shoes dance and it frightens your... ***

Frank plays his viola all of the time
Who says a poem always has to... ****

Post Office
**conut
***granny
**** have a similar sound at the end of the line as it had at the end of the line before

POEM FOR SALE

Apply Roger Stevens

Poem For Sale
(One careful owner)
With simile
(as lucky as a dime)
Two exquisite
And erudite adjectives
And one rhyme

Going
For a song

GET YOUR POEMS HERE

Roll up. Roll up
Get your poems here
They're lovely

Four verses a fiver
Can't say fairer than that
Couplets – a pound a pair
Free metaphor with every purchase
And I'm cutting off my nose to spite my face

Roll up. Roll up
Get your poems here
They're lovely

Bespoke Ballads
Made-to-measure Quatrains
Genuine Haiku
Guaranteed all the way from Japan
Written on the slopes of Kilimanjaro
Seventeen pence a syllable
That's seventeen times seventeen...
Tell you what
Call it three quid
And I'll throw in two extra syllables

Roll up. Roll up
Get your poems here
They're lovely

Poems sublime
Poems that rhyme
And rap poems
Don't forget we gift wrap
And we gift wrap rap
All poems ready to take away

Roll up. Roll up
Get your poems here
They're lovely

ARE YOU FAMOUS?

On a scale of one to Michael Rosen
I'm probably a seven
On a scale of soft to very loud
I'm probably eleven
On a scale of one to Einstein
I'm probably one-and-a-half
On a scale of groan to hysteria
I'm probably a laugh
On a scale of one to infinity
I'm a meagre sixty-one
On a scale of A to Z
I hover at F for Fun
On a scale of amoeba to gorilla
I'm sitting on top of the tree
On the scale of now till the end of time
I'll soon be history

GHERKIN CAR

I am the Picasso of Poetry
Ear nose blue pink eye spoon
Burnt ochre
Sienna
Five plums a tenner
A six-year-old child could write this
Exclamation mark
Wonky donkey
Bob

HALF A DOZEN SENYRU

1
Dads at the school gate
Starlings in the autumn sky
Heading home to roost

2
Hippopotamus
It's a wonder how you squeezed
Into this small space

3
If a poem has
Just sixteen syllables
Is it a lowku?

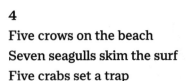

4
Five crows on the beach
Seven seagulls skim the surf
Five crabs set a trap

5
Grey clouds gathering
The boat is two hours late
The scent of thyme

6
Around the corner
Sweep five sleek black limousines
Moosh, spelt in flowers

Senryū is a form of Japanese poetry similar to haiku in construction, with three lines of seventeen syllables. But while haiku are serious and tend to be about nature, senryū tend to be about human foibles and can be witty or funny. And, as with haiku, they shouldn't have titles.

MORE HAIKU-STYLE FUN

1
Those less able Japanese scholars
Often wrote poems with exactly seventeen words
But they fell from favour

2
When I write haiku
I always seem to have one
syllable left o

ver

EXACTLY SEVENTEEN SILLY BALLS

THE POETRY GRAND NATIONAL

The poems line up
They're under starter's orders
They're off

Adverb leaps gracefully over the first fence
Followed by Adjective
A sleek, grey poem

Simile is overtaking on the outside
Like a pebble skimming the water

Half-way round the course
And Hyperbole is gaining on the leaders
Travelling at a million miles an hour

Adverb strides smoothly into first place

Haiku had good odds
But is far behind – and falls
At the last sylla-
ble

And as they flash past the winning post
The crowd is cheering
The winner is
Personification
Who quietly takes a bow

A POEM'S PLEA

I'm a lonely little poem
I want to be read out
Not just sit in a book
In the dark, all filled with doubt

Wondering if I'll be chosen next
To take the stage
Or if I'll be for evermore
Just words upon a page

Yes, I'm a little poem
And I want to be a star
Now you're going to close the page I'm on...

Admit it...

Yes, you are...

THE WORLD
OF THE WILD

LOW-FLYING RABBITS AHEAD

Watch out for obstreperous elephants
Or fidgety fleas in your bed
There's a bear on your chair – don't stare! Beware!
Low-flying rabbits ahead

Be warned! Argumentative aardvarks
And the tigers haven't been fed
When in doubt you must shout, There be dragons –
    watch out!
Low-flying rabbits ahead

Caution – cantankerous catfish
There's a dodo called Fred in the shed
And the mad fortune-teller says, Take your umbrella!
Low-flying rabbits ahead

Be prepared for the lemur's cruel laughter
Don't forget what the old tortoise said
Life is fun. When in doubt – don't worry about
Those low-flying rabbits ahead

THE BROWN BEAR

In the dark wood
In a clearing
Sleeps a brown bear
Dreaming, dreaming

His skin is furless
His paws are clawless
He walks into the city
Lawless, lawless

The moon is hidden
The clouds are weeping
A princess slumbers
Sleeping, sleeping

The thief creeps through
The royal bedroom
And steals her ruby
A priceless heirloom

The ruby glows
With fire and lightning
A spell is cast
So frightening, frightening

The thief grows fur
His body thickens
His hands grow claws
He sickens, sickens

Beneath the black sky
Thunder rumbles
Into the dark wood
He stumbles, stumbles

For in the ruby,
Gleaming, gleaming
A wizard's mind
Is scheming, scheming

Now, in the dark wood
In a clearing
Sleeps a brown bear
Dreaming, dreaming

DRAGON LOVE POEM

When you smile
the room lights up

and I have to call
the fire brigade

MAYFLY'S DIARY

Monday October 1st

The sun's coming up
I'm born
I'm alive
Look at the grass
The sun
The sky
Made a new friend
Together we fly
Sun's going down
Must go
Goodbye

MOSQUITO

Oi

Mosi

Quit,

Mosi,

Quit!

I included this poem because it's a fun and quite tricky poem to write. Have you noticed that the only letters I've used in the poem are the letters in the poem's title?

ESCAPE PLAN

As I, Stegosaurus,
stand motionless
in the Natural History Museum,
I am secretly planning
my escape.

At noon
Pterodactyl
will cause a diversion
by wheeling around the museum's high ceilings
and diving at the curators and museum staff,
while I
quietly slip out of the fire exit
and melt
into the Kensington crowds.

FUNNY HA HA

NOT MUCH TO LOOK AT

My name is R2D2
I'm not much to look at for sure
I don't have the figure of a 6PO-7
Nor the face of a ZKO-4

I don't have the elegance of a CP3-O
And my manners aren't neat and precise
I can't speak every language under the sun
But I have saved the galaxy – twice

THE MONSTER THAT ATE THE UNIVERSE

I began with a pancake
But why stop there?
So I ate the spoon
And the table and chair
What's my name?
The Monster that Ate the Universe

I ate all the cutlery
I ate the cheese grater
The cooker, the microwave
The refrigerator
What's my name?
The Monster that Ate the Universe

I wolfed down the kitchen
The dining room, too
I slurped up the bathroom
Including the loo
What's my name?
The Monster that Ate the Universe

I chewed up the house
I gulped it all down
I ate the whole street
Then I swallowed the town
What's my name?
The Monster that Ate the Universe

I devoured the country
Then what do you think?
I drank all the ocean
I needed a drink
What's my name?
The Monster that Ate the Universe

I consumed the Earth, the planets, the sun
I was still feeling peckish
And having such fun
What's my name?
The Monster that Ate the Universe

So I gorged on the galaxy
Then the galaxy next door
I was still feeling hungry
So I gobbled up more
What's my name?
The Monster that Ate the Universe

I dined on them all
As the prophets all feared
Then I swallowed myself
And just disappeared

In the silence that followed
A little bird sang
Then nothing. Just silence.
And a very big

BANG!

REFLECTION

As the ball

Hit the bat

The bat

Reflected upon

Its defective

Sonar

ITEMS IN THE EDWARD LEAR MUSEUM

A runcible spoon and ticket (first class)
Thirty nine bottles of Ring Bo Ree
A scarlet flannel, a crockery jar
A sieve that has travelled the Western Sea
Some oblong oysters (just their shells) and the hat
Of Mr Quangle Wangle Quee
And in pride of place, in a crumbobblious case
A branch from the old Bong Tree
Some waterproof clothes, the beard and a nose
And a branch of the old Bong Tree

Please read some poems by Edward Lear,
especially his limericks, for which he is
famous. I think you'll enjoy them.

Picture by Edward Lear from A Book of Nonsense 1846

HALLOWE'EN

Darren's got a pumpkin
Hollowed out a treat
He put it in the window
It scared half the street

I wish I had a pumpkin
But I've not and it's a shame
I've got a scary carrot
But it's not the same

TRICK OR TREAT

As we lurch along the darkened street
This spooky Hallowe'en
Freddy is dressed as Frankenstein
His face a sickly green
Darren is dressed as a mummy
Bandaged from head to feet
Sarah is a scary ghost
Wrapped up in a sheet
I am dressed as Dracula
My cape is red and black
But I wish I knew who the Zombie was
Creeping along at the back

This is probably my favourite poem to perform., Here's what you do. Read the poem as if you were walking along the street one Hallowe'en night, being followed by your friends dressed as scary characters. Start in your usual loud, clear voice. But as the poem progresses get quieter and quieter until you get to the last line. Pause, just before you whisper "Creeping along at the back." You'll find that your audience get quieter too, and this helps build the tension. Then, after pausing for just a couple of heartbeats, shout out BOO! In a very loud voice.

CHUTNEY

Sixteen jars
Of tomato chutney
Sit in the cupboard
Chuckling

THE HOLDING YOUR BREATH CONTEST

We held a Hold Your Breath contest,

Me, Sammy, Sean and Sid.

Sid held his breath for a fortnight.

We're going to miss that kid.

SOME OF MY FAVOURITES

MISSING THE BOAT

The Woebegoing cried big fat tears
as the animals entered the Ark.
He'd been packing his case for thirteen years,
at first for a bit of a lark.
But now, as the animals boarded the ship,
he sat on the bank and bit his lip.

For thirteen years he'd searched the land,
looking for a mate.
For thirteen years he'd sifted sand,
but now it was too late.
He rang his bell,
sang
a farewell song
and the Woebegoing
was the Woebegone.

WHAT SHALL I CALL IT?

I need a name for this poem
Has anyone got a clue?
It needs to be funny, slightly surreal
You know, seen from an odd point of view

For example Low-flying Rabbits Ahead
Beware - High-flying Hares
Aardvark Through the Looking Glass
Why the Wow Wow Got Stuck on the Stairs

The Fiddler Spider's Party
When the Cheetah Raced the Sloth
There's a Halibut in the Underpass
Two Many Coypu Spoil the Broth

What News of the Lemmings?
Confusing a Spink with a Snipe
Playing Basketball with a Bulldog
When the Whiting Needs a Wipe

The Twelve Starfish of the Zodiac
The Secret of Prairie Dog's Box
Why Alligators love Elevators
Why Otters Don't Wear Socks

I need a name for this poem
What to call it – I haven't a clue
I think I'll just call it – What Shall I Call It?
And leave the decision to you

THE WINNING GOAL

When I scored the winning goal
I had never felt so alone
The crowd went crazy, on their feet
But my heart sank like a stone
They say that scoring is marvellous
The best feeling that's ever been known
But it's hard to take
When you make a mistake
And the back of the net
Is your own

NEVER TRUST A LEMON

Never trust a lemon
It's a melon in disguise
Never trust potatoes
With shifty eyes
Never trust a radish
It repeats all that it hears
Never trust an onion
It will all end in tears

SIX EGGS

Six eggs
Hide in their dark
Cocoons
Nursing
Sunshine

EXTRACT FROM A SHEPHERD'S DIARY

A long time ago in
Bethlehem. December 23rd

It's freezing up here on the hill.
Nothing to do
but gaze up at the stars
once the sheep have all been fed.

Tonight's my last night,
then back to the day shift, thank God.
Tomorrow night
I'll be tucked up warm in bed.

ON A POET'S DAY OFF

On a poet's day off
Haikus can have a couple of
Extra syllables

On a poet's day off
Moons rhyme with July
And never wane or wax

On a poet's day off
Clouds blow across the sky
Daffodils grow in clumps
The breeze doesn't sigh

On a poet's day off
Words take wing
And similes can have a rest
Like
As not

A poet's day off?
There's no such thing!

THE MOST IMPORTANT RAP

(for Denis Waitley)

I am an astronaut
I circle the stars
I walk on the moon
I travel to Mars
I'm brave and tall
There is nothing I fear
And I am the most important person here

I am a teacher
I taught you it all
I taught you why your
spaceship doesn't fall
If you couldn't read or write
where would you be?
The most important person here is me

Who are you kidding?
Are you taking the mick?
Who makes you better
when you're feeling sick?
I am a doctor
and I'm always on call
And I am more important than you all

But I'm your mother
Don't forget me
If it wasn't for your mother
where would you be?
I washed your nappies
and changed your vest
I'm the most important
and Mummy knows best

I am a child
and the future I see
and there'd be no future
if it wasn't for me
I hold the safety
of the planet in my hand
I'm the most important
and you'd better understand

Now just hold on
I've a message for you all
Together we stand
and divided we fall
So let's make a circle
and all remember this
Who's the most important?

EVERYBODY IS!

ABOUT THE POET

 **ROGER STEVENS** is one of the UK's best-loved children's poets. He has had more than forty books published and appears on television and radio, sharing his joy in poetry with thousands of children and grown-ups. His poetry performances and workshops are hugely popular at festivals, in schools and libraries.

His internationally acclaimed website, **www.poetryzone.co.uk**, has been helping children to write, and giving useful tips to teachers, for nearly twenty-five years. He is a National Poetry Day Ambassador and works with various organisations promoting the teaching of poetry in schools and colleges.

Roger writes poetry for adults and is a musician with several solo albums to his credit. He lives in Brighton and France, with his wife and very shy dog called Jasper.

ABOUT THE ILLUSTRATOR

 **MIKE SMITH** graduated with an MA in Children's Book Illustration from Cambridge School of Art in 2011. In 2010 he won the Macmillan Prize for children's book illustration, having been a runner-up the year before.

His picture books include *The Hundred Decker Bus* and *The Hundred Decker Rocket*, published by Macmillan. He has also produced strips for The Phoenix comic, including the long-running *Planet of the Shapes*, and illustrated several of the *First Names* biography series.

Mike is happiest writing and drawing stories where humour grows from character — the more ridiculous the better! His main influences and childhood favourites were Richard Scarry, Hergé and Charles Schultz.

He lives in Wales with his family, a dog and a growing collection of pencils.

ALSO BY ROGER STEVENS

Published by Otter-Barry Books

ISBN 978-1-91095-965-7

ISBN 978-1-91095-989-3